money
money

WE ALL NEED IT—AT LEAST, ENOUGH TO GET BY.
SO HOW DO YOU EARN IT, SAVE IT, AND SPEND IT?

True or False?

1 **The best way to get a job is to wait for one to fall into your lap.**

2 **A checking account is a detailed description of a hockey play.**

3 **An IRA is a government organization that collects taxes.**

4 **APR are the initials of the last winner on *American Idol*.**

5 **It's okay to pay credit cards late once in a while.**

Answer: If you answered true to any of these questions, you could stand to learn more about money. But don't panic! This book is your go-to guide to handling your financial life.

Photographs © 2008: Alamy Images: 25 (Frances M. Roberts), 58 (Steven Widoff), 31 (David Young-Wolff); Corbis Images: 40 (Cameron), 78 (Comstock), 103 (Hill Street Studios/Stock This Way), 100 (Image Source), 4 bottom, 42 (Sean Justice), 81 (Simon Marcus), 64 (Rob Melnychuk/Brand X), 61 (Mika/zefa), 35 (Jose Luis Pelaez, Inc.), 77 (Darius Ramazani/zefa), 50 (Neil C. Robinson), 96 (Chuck Savage), 51 (Visuals Unlimited); Getty Images: 63 (Anne Ackermann), 13 (Benelux Press), 6 (Ryan McVay), 68 (Dave Nagel), 83 (Stephanie Rausser); Image Source/Image Source Pink: 80; Monty Stilson: cover; The Image Works: 4 top, 14 (John Birdsall), 45, 47 (Bob Daemmrich); VEER: 54 (Alloy Photography), 16 (Blend Images Photography), 91 (Digital Vision Photography).

Cover design: Marie O'Neill
Book production: The Design Lab
CHOICES editor: Bob Hugel

Library of Congress Cataloging-in-Publication Data
Denega, Danielle.
Smart money : how to manage your cash / Danielle Denega.
    p. cm.—(Choices)
Includes bibliographical references and index.
 ISBN-13: 978-0-531-18847-7 (lib. bdg.)   978-0-531-14772-6 (pbk.)
 ISBN-10: 0-531-18847-7 (lib. bdg.)   0-531-14772-X (pbk.)
 1. Finance, Personal. 2. Teenagers—Finance, Personal. 3. Money. I.
Title. II. Title: Smart money.
 HG179.D43 2008
 332.02400835—dc22   2007011288

1 2 3 4 5 6 7 8 9 10 R 17 16 15 14 13 12 11 10 09 08

How to manage your cash

smart money

Danielle Denega

Franklin Watts

AN IMPRINT OF SCHOLASTIC INC.
NEW YORK • TORONTO • LONDON • AUCKLAND • SYDNEY
MEXICO CITY • NEW DELHI • HONG KONG
DANBURY, CONNECTICUT

money,
money,
money,
money!

money, money, money, mo-ney!

"I NEVER REALLY THOUGHT FAR ENOUGH AHEAD."

Mark's Story

"I never really thought far enough ahead to realize that I could do something better with my money—something smarter."

Last summer, Mark had a huge bar mitzvah celebration. His family and friends bombarded him with monetary gifts. "I had a mountain of envelopes to open. It was awesome!" he recalls. "I cashed all the checks I got and stuck the money in a box in my bedroom for a couple of weeks."

This sounds like a dream come true: money for nothing! But the hitch was that Mark had little experience dealing with money.

Mark explains, "By the time school started, I felt really flush. So I began spending the money. I ate out a lot, bought computer games and hockey equipment. The money ran out really quickly, and I felt pretty stupid that I'd spent it all and didn't have much to show for it. I could have saved it . . . for something worthwhile—like a car or something. Plus my parents were not too happy with me."

Mark came into a lot of money but didn't know what to do with it when he had it. Instead of banking it or **investing** it, Mark quickly spent his cash on small items. "No one ever told me that I could earn more money from my money. So I wasted it because it was there. I never really thought far enough ahead to realize that I could do something better with my money—something smarter."

18%

Eighteen percent of teenagers consider themselves "clueless" or "not very smart" about how to spend, save, and budget money.

Why Do We Need Money?

If Mark's story sounds familiar to you, don't be worried. You're not alone. Many people don't know much about money: how to get it, how to save it, or how to spend it wisely.

So why is it so important to understand money? Simply put, money is a key part of life. Money buys you the stuff you need and want, and without it, life is a lot harder.

Stop for a moment and think about all the things around you that cost money. Money paid for the roof over your head, the food in the fridge, and the bed you rolled out of this morning.

Now take a moment to think about some of the other things money got you: your computer, your MP3 player, your video game console, your jeans, your TV . . . the list could go on forever. And imagine living without your cell phone. Hard to imagine, isn't it?

THESE things don't come FREE

These things don't come free. In fact, they don't even come cheap much of the time. So if you like having nice gadgets, wearing nice clothes, or even just eating every day, you need to have a basic understanding of money.

MONEY
and
MINTS

The origin of the word *money* comes from the Latin word *moneta*, meaning "mint" or "coin." In the early days of Rome, the Roman mint was located in the temple dedicated to Juno Moneta, the queen of the gods.

Mint? Isn't that a candy? Well, yes. And it's a plant. But in this sense of the word, *mint* refers to a place where coins, medals, or tokens are made.

Where Your Money Goes

To begin understanding money, you first have to understand how much you've got and what you're using it for. As a 21st-century teenager, you have access to more money than teenagers ever had before.

Between allowances, gifts, and income from chores and part-time jobs, teenagers are raking in the dough like never before. According to one poll, most teens spend about $20 per week ($80 per month), and many spend double that amount.

But in the same poll, teens said they had bigger plans for their cash, like buying a car.

WHAT
are teens buying with their cash?

Top items teens last bought with their own money

1	Clothes
2	Food
3	Candy
3	Soda or soft drinks
4	Salty snacks (i.e., chips)
4	CDs or recorded music
5	Lunch
6	Shoes
7	Video games
8	Jewelry
9	Magazines
10	Ice cream

Source: http://www.magazine.org/
content/files/teenprofile04.pdf

As Mark learned the hard way, when you have a lot of money, it can disappear quickly. "I couldn't believe how fast and easy it is to spend a lot of money. One minute, I was thinking that it would last me years. But then I got trigger-happy, and it was gone. I didn't save a dime. I'm pretty mad at myself for that."

More than half of teens put some money into savings. It's obvious that spending money is fun, and saving it ... well, not so much. However, saving money is one of the most important things you'll ever do. Sounds dramatic, but it's true!

In 2005, teens in the United States spent about $160 billion on clothing, music, technology, food, and entertainment.

When you save your money, you can use it later to buy things you want (like DVDs and clothes), as well as to pay for things you need (like college or a car). And if you're *really* smart, you can make your money earn more money.

Basically, making smart decisions about your money enables you to have it when you truly need it.

A TIME **TO** SAVE

How important is saving money to teens?

92%

Ninety-two percent of American teens think it's necessary to have good money habits to be successful in life.

20%

But at the same time, 20 percent of American teens think they are young enough that saving money isn't that important.

in the
money

in the
money

"I WORKED AS OFTEN AS I COULD."

Malcolm's Story

Malcolm, a high-school junior, was used to his parents getting him the things he wanted. That changed when he became old enough to earn money. "My parents were starting to give me a hard time whenever I asked them for money. They told me to get a job. So I did."

"My friend's dad owns his own business," he continued, "so I asked his father if I could work for him during the summer. He said that both me and his son should work for him. We were pretty happy about that idea."

Malcolm began working for his friend's father, stuffing envelopes all summer. "He told me I could work as many hours as I wanted, within reason. As long as I was busy stuffing and sealing those envelopes the whole time, he'd keep paying me. So I worked as often as I could. My hands were all covered in bandages from the paper cuts I got—I stuffed a lot of envelopes!"

Malcolm stuffed so many envelopes, in fact, that by the end of that summer, he had about $2,000 tucked away.

TEENAGERS
are most likely to have a job that involves **MANUAL LABOR (32%)** or **FOOD SERVICE (30%)**.

Money Doesn't Grow on Trees!

Now you have a better understanding of why money is important. So what's the easiest way to make sure you always have enough of it? Ding, ding, ding! You guessed it—working.

Reality check: To get the goods, you're going to need a source of income—a job. It's a scary word, but one with which you should get comfortable. In fact, about half of all teens get their money from having jobs (such as baby-sitting) and from doing household chores for cash.

But before you go out and get a job, take a look at your life. Do you have enough free time? Don't cheat yourself out of time for family, friends, homework, sports, and other important activities. Okay, now let's take a look at the working world: how to get a job, how to keep a job, and how to make sure your hours and pay are what they should be.

REALITY CHECK To get the goods, you're going to need a source of income—a job.

ALLOWANCES

and gifts

Approximately one half of teens are given much of their money. Many young people are given money as gifts, such as for a birthday. And many other teens are given a weekly or monthly allowance—a set amount of cash that is theirs to spend on what they choose.

Source: USA Weekend Magazine, May 2, 1999

45% of teens get no weekly allowance

17% of teens have an allowance of more than $20 a week

17% of teens are given $10 to $20 each week

16% of teens receive between $5 and $10 per week

5% of teens get less than $5 a week as an allowance

Getting a Job

You've realized that jobs equal money, and money equals all the stuff you want to buy. So you need a job. How are you supposed to get one?

The first thing to do is find places to apply. The Internet and the newspaper are great places to find Help Wanted listings. Check out groovejobs.com and the classified ads in your local paper or on their Web site.

Another way to get a job is to pick where you want to work and contact people there, even if you don't know that they are hiring. It never hurts to ask. This is exactly what Malcolm did when he wanted to find a job, and it worked out really well for him. "I knew my friend's dad had a business and that he was a pretty okay guy, so I figured it wouldn't be bad working for him. I think he was impressed when I asked him if I could work for him. I think it's part of the reason he hired me. I showed him I really wanted it."

When you show up at a more traditional business looking for work, such as a restaurant or store, be prepared to fill out an application. An application is a form provided by employers. You fill it out in order to tell the employer a little about yourself: where you go to school, if you've had a job before, and when you are available to work.

JOB APPLICATION

Personal Information ....

Education ....

Position Applied For ....

Old Employment Information ....

References ....

Job applications ask for a lot of information. And they need to be complete and accurate. So it's a really smart move to show up prepared. Have names, phone numbers, and addresses with you, so that you can copy them onto the application correctly.

Also, be sure to write clearly and neatly. Take it slow so you don't make any errors. Use a pen with blue or black ink—that looks the most professional. And when you have finished the application, go back and check it carefully. Make sure you spelled everything correctly and that you gave accurate phone numbers and dates.

Other Tips for Getting the Job You Want

Before you head out the door to look for jobs, stop for one second and look in the mirror. Do you like what you see? If not, pull yourself together! Shower, brush your teeth, and put on clean, nice clothes before going to meet with any employer. And when you get there, stand up straight and speak clearly and confidently.

Finally, after you've applied for a job and spoken with a manager, follow up. This is probably the most important part of getting a job. Seriously! After you've left, put in a call, send an e-mail, or mail a letter thanking the employer for spending time with you. This goes a long way in showing employers that you mean business.

DO YOUR
homework

Executive recruiter Carlos Silva-Craig says, "Do some research about the company at which you are applying. Make sure you know a little about it so that you can speak knowledgeably in an interview."

Types of Jobs for Teens

Now that you know the basics about finding a job, let's look at some options for the types of jobs you can get. Because you're still in school, you have two opportunities: part-time jobs and summer jobs.

Part-time jobs require you to work a few hours after school and/or on the weekends. Summer jobs may require you to work more hours because most teens aren't in school then. Often, teenagers will work a lot during the summer, save the money they earn, and use it to pay for expenses during the school year.

Here are some job suggestions to get you on your way to financial freedom from your parents:

OUTDOOR MAINTENANCE WORK

WHAT'S INVOLVED: Shoveling snow, mowing lawns, raking up leaves, pulling weeds

HOW MUCH IT PAYS: Varies, but you could ask for as much as $10–$20/hour

HOW TO GET THIS JOB: These are tasks people will gladly pay you to do. Knock on your neighbors' doors, especially after a snowfall or when the leaves are piling up. Post signs around town with your name and phone number. Good places to post flyers are hardware and home improvement stores.

PERKS: You might get tips.

RETAIL

WHAT'S INVOLVED: Helping customers at local stores, such as a clothing store, comic book shop, movie theater, or ice cream stand

HOW MUCH IT PAYS: Generally minimum wage or slightly higher

HOW TO GET THIS JOB: Check the local newspaper's classified ads, where retail businesses often advertise. Walk or drive from business to business. A stroll through the mall or strip mall is a good option, too. You'll more than likely find at least one business with a Help Wanted sign in its window.

PERKS: You might get freebies or discounts.

SITTING

WHAT'S INVOLVED: Baby-sitting, pet-sitting, or house-sitting

HOW MUCH IT PAYS: It varies, but you could start off asking for $7–$10/hour.

HOW TO GET THIS JOB: Ask neighbors and family friends with small children if they need help. Posting flyers advertising your services is also smart. Good places to hang baby-sitting ads include anywhere people take their kids, from the grocery store to the YMCA, or at local schools. For pet-sitting, post flyers at vet offices, in dog parks, at pet stores, and at grooming shops.

PERKS: You can probably do homework, read, or surf the Web when the kids (dogs, gerbils, whatever!) are asleep.

TUTOR

WHAT'S INVOLVED: If you are good at a particular subject, you can earn big bucks helping others get good at it, too. Consider tutoring people of all ages: little kids, your peers, or even adults who are trying to learn English as a second language, for example.

HOW MUCH IT PAYS: It varies, but you could ask for $10–$50/hour.

HOW TO GET THIS JOB: Posting flyers is also good for this type of service. Schools, pediatricians' offices, and the library are all good places to hang them.

PERKS: You're practicing your skills in the subject, and you're gaining teaching experience.

SPORTS AND RECREATION

WHAT'S INVOLVED: Caddy at the local golf course, referee or coach little kids' teams, or be a lifeguard. Use your athletic interests and abilities to make money!

HOW MUCH IT PAYS: It varies widely.

HOW TO GET THIS JOB: Check the local classified ads for job openings. Some organizations will post ads. Or call local sports organizations—such as the Little League, the YMCA, recreation centers, and country clubs—to see if they are hiring. Most lifeguard jobs will require you to take a first aid and CPR class before starting.

PERKS: You'll likely get in shape, or at least get some fresh air, along with that nice cash.

CAMPS

WHAT'S INVOLVED: A great summer job option is working at a camp. They need everything from counselors to groundskeepers to dishwashers.

HOW MUCH IT PAYS: Usually minimum wage and can include room and board if it is an overnight camp.

HOW TO GET THIS JOB: Contact local camps by phone or e-mail to see if they are hiring for the summer. Look into this early though, as spots may be taken if you wait until school ends.

PERKS: A lot of times, you can stay at the camp all summer and, in your downtime, chill with the other teens who work there.

GET CREATIVE

WHAT'S INVOLVED: You have skills that are bankable, even though you may not realize it. Maybe you're talented with computers and could be the local IT guy or help people set up Web sites for themselves. Perhaps you are a fabulous knitter and could sell scarves to shops in your town. You might be a killer musician, so why not give lessons to others? Or if you're into photography, you could take photos for special events.

HOW MUCH IT PAYS: The sky is the limit!

HOW TO GET THIS JOB: Post flyers advertising your services. Or approach local businesses to see if they'd be interested in selling your goods.

PERKS: You can make your own hours and do something you love at the same time.

YOUNG
entrepreneurs

Take a cue from some of these young entrepreneurs when thinking of job options. They got really creative, and it paid off big.

- **Elise and Evan Macmillan** are cofounders of the Chocolate Farm, a maker of custom gourmet chocolates. Evan was only 13 and Elisa was only 10 when they started their business. In 1999, the Chocolate Farm received an Ernst & Young Entrepreneur of the Year Award, and it was rated the top youth food business in the United States in 2001.

- **Ben Casnocha** started Comcate, a San Francisco–based software company, at age 12. Comcate's annual revenues are about $750,000.

- When he was 12 years old, **Ben Cathers** started a Web marketing and advertising firm geared toward teenagers. In 2000, when Ben was only 15, the *Silicon Alley Reporter* named his firm one of the "Top 12 companies in Silicon Alley to look out for."

5

The Five Worst Jobs for Teens

The National Consumers League has pegged these jobs as the most dangerous for young people. So in your quest to find a job, think twice about the following:

1. **Delivery and other driving**, including operating or riding on forklifts and other motorized equipment
2. **Working alone** in cash-based businesses such as convenience stores, gasoline stations, and fast-food establishments
3. **Traveling youth crews:** selling candy, magazine subscriptions, and other consumer goods on street corners, in strange neighborhoods, in distant cities, and across state lines
4. **Cooking:** exposure to hot oil and grease, hot water and steam, and hot cooking surfaces
5. **Construction**, including work at heights and in contact with electrical power

Source: life.familyeducation.com/summer-jobs/jobs-and-chores/29669.html?detoured=1

Brian's Story

Brian, now age 16, remembers, "My first job was making truffles in a gourmet candy store. I was only thirteen. I wasn't supposed to be working yet, but no one asked about my age. They paid me for every dozen truffles I made, which I also don't think they were supposed to be doing. And they made me sit in the walk-in refrigerator while I did it, so the chocolate wouldn't melt. It was freezing!

When my friend's mother found out what was going on where I was working, she called my parents and let them know. After that, I didn't work at the candy store much longer! The next summer, I turned 14, and my parents let me get another job. But they paid much closer attention that time."

Brian was too young to be working at 13. The company broke the law by hiring him, and it is illegal for anyone under the age of 16 to work in a freezer or cooler.

Before you begin your promising career, make sure you're aware of the types of work young people are legally allowed to do and what hours are okay when school is in session versus weekends and summertime.

Work Rules and Regulations for Young People

If you are younger than 14, U.S. law says that you're not old enough to do most types of work. You may do things such as baby-sitting or yard work. You may also work as an actor or performer in motion pictures, television, theater, or radio. You may work in a business solely owned or operated by your parents, including a farm.

If you are 14 or 15 years of age, you also may work in an office, grocery store, retail store, restaurant, movie theater, baseball park, amusement park, or gasoline service station.

If you are age 14 or 15, there are laws about the hours you can work.

- **You are allowed to work only before or after school.**
- **You can work only between the hours of 7 A.M. and 7 P.M. during the school year. In the summer, you can work as late as 9 P.M.**
- **You cannot work more than three hours a day if it's a school day and eighteen hours per week during a school week.**
- **You also cannot work more than eight hours on a non-school day or more than forty hours in a non-school week.**

Minimum Wage

In the United States, there is a minimum wage. That's the lowest amount of money that employers can legally pay employees. The federal government sets a minimum wage for the whole country. But each state also has minimum wage laws, which may call for higher wages than the federal government. For information about current minimum wage rules, go to the Department of Labor's Web site: www.dol.gov/esa/minwage/america.htm. Make sure you know what the minimum wages are, so you can keep from getting cheated!

Once you turn 16, you can work in any job or occupation that has not been declared hazardous by the U.S. Department of Labor. You can also work as many hours and days as an adult. At 18, you are considered an adult, so you are free to do pretty much any type of work you desire. The child labor rules no longer apply to you.

Keep in mind that different rules apply to farms, and individual states may have stricter rules, especially for jobs that deal with selling or serving alcohol. Check out the Department of Labor's Web site to get more information: www.dol.gov.

Keeping Your Job

If you've landed a job, you're doing something right, so nice work. But, unfortunately, the effort doesn't end there. You have to take steps to hold on to that job.

1. **Show up: Be on time, every time.**

2. **Be a diligent worker: Get as much done as you can while you are there.**

3. **Have a good attitude: Do your job with a smile. A grumpy attitude doesn't help the time go any faster.**

4. **Represent yourself and your employer well: Dress and speak appropriately. Treat managers, co-workers, and customers with respect.**

You're Not the Boss of Me!

Some bosses are hated simply because they are the boss. Other bosses are just the grumpy type. People like this can be tricky to deal with. You need to look out for yourself, but you also need to be respectful of your boss's authority.

At work, if you don't play by the rules of the game, there are consequences. If you're scolded for not fulfilling your job requirements, you have no one to blame but yourself. But if you feel your boss is being unfair, there are a few strategies for working it out.

- Try talking it out. No matter what, be polite!
- If talking to your boss doesn't make things better, try talking to another manager.
- Talk to your boss's manager or the human resources department. But be careful! Your boss may find out, and that could make things worse.
- Just deal with it! If the situation isn't too bad, just accept the fact that life is sometimes unfair.
- If the situation is really terrible and you cannot change it, quit the job and look for a new one.

Understanding Your Paycheck

A first glance at a paycheck can leave you feeling totally confused. Your pay stub will show you all the deductions from your paycheck. Here's a sample pay stub and some basics to help you decipher it.

Pizza Shack
1234 Marketplace Street
Hometown, NY 12345

Employee Number:	94-4455667
Social Security Number:	XXX-XX-0789
Marital Status:	SINGLE
Number of Allowances:	00
Rate:	10.00

Earnings Statement

| Pay Period: | 4/16/2007 to 4/30/2007 |
| Pay Date: | 4/30/2007 |

Zoey Quigley
678 Residence Ave
Hometown, NY 12345

Hours of Earnings			
Description	Hours	This Period	Year-To-Date
Regular	20.00	200.00	1770.00

Taxes and Deductions		
Description	This Period	Year-To-Date
FICA	15.00	135.41
Federal	2.00	59.68
NY state	9.21	40.32

Gross Pay Year To Date	Gross Pay This Period	Total Deductions This Period	Net Pay This Period
$1,770.00	$200.00	$26.21	$173.79

Gross pay: The total amount of money you earned before any money has been deducted.

Net pay: This is the amount of money you really take home.

Federal income tax: Money withheld to pay for national programs. The amount taken is determined by how much money you earn and how you filled out your W-4 form when you started your job.

FICA: FICA is short for Federal Insurance Compensation Act. In other words, it's Social Security, our country's national retirement system. It provides for retirees in two ways: (1) after-retirement income—6.2 percent of your pay goes for that; (2) after-retirement health care—1.45 percent of your pay goes for that.

State income tax: Money withheld to cover income tax you owe the state. Some states don't have state income tax, and the ones that do have different tax rates.

City income tax: Money withheld to cover income tax you owe the city. Not all cities have this.

SDI (state disability insurance): Money withheld to provide workers with partial pay during serious illnesses and injuries. Only a handful of states have this.

Sarah's Story

According to 18-year-old Sarah, "Getting a paycheck rules ... until you actually read it and see that you aren't getting as much money as you thought you would. When I saw how much money was being taken out of my checks, I freaked. I was so mad.

"But my parents explained what all the deductions were and that there's no way of getting around them. But when you really think about it, our taxes and stuff go toward good causes, and everyone pays them, so it's not like you're getting ripped off while everybody else is getting their full earnings."

"When I saw how much money was being taken out of my checks, I freaked. I was so mad."

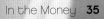

Tax Basics

Now that you understand more about taxes, let's take a closer look at what they mean for you as a teenager. Here are a few basics to put you in the know when it comes to paying taxes.

1. **Working means paying taxes.** If you receive a paycheck from a company, taxes will be deducted from your pay. If you make over a certain amount in a given year (for 2006, that amount was $5,150), you will have to file an income tax form and pay those taxes, too.

2. **You can do your own taxes.** They aren't that complicated, and an adult can guide you.

3. **Just because you employ yourself doesn't mean you don't have to pay taxes.** The money you earn doing things such as pet-sitting, baby-sitting, or mowing lawns is considered income by the U.S. government. You have to pay self-employment taxes on it if the amount is above what is set for that year. For example, in 2006, if you made more than $400 from being self-employed, you had to file a tax return.

4. Forms may equal more $ for you in the end.

As a young adult, you may not always have to file a tax return, but it may be a good idea anyway. Let's say you worked part time for a company and only earned a small amount of money. Federal income taxes were taken out of your pay, but you could get some money back as a tax refund.

Schedule C form: A tax form on which profit and loss from an unincorporated business is listed. If you have been doing self-employment work, such as shoveling snow, you will have to fill out one of these.

Tax Forms
EXPLAINED

W-4 Form: A tax form that allows your employer to calculate the amount of tax to withhold from your pay. When you get a job, you will need to fill out one of these. On line 5, your total number allowances will be zero (unless you are living on your own or married).

Form **W-4**

Department of the Treasury
Internal Revenue Service

Employee's Withholding Allowance Certificate

OMB No. 1545-0074

2007

▶ **Whether you are entitled to claim a certain number of allowances or exemption from withholding is subject to review by the IRS. Your employer may be required to send a copy of this form to the IRS.**

1 Type or print your first name and middle initial.

Zoey

Last name

Quigley

2 Your social security number

123 : **45** : **6789**

Home address (number and street or rural route)

678 Residence Avenue

Hometown, NY, 12345

3 ☒ Single ☐ Married ☐ Married, but withhold at higher Single rate.

Note. If married, but legally separated, or spouse is a nonresident alien, check the "Single" box.

4 If your last name differs from that shown on your social security card, check here. You must call 1-800-772-1213 for a replacement card. ▶ ☐

5 Total number of allowances you are claiming (from line **H** above **or** from the applicable worksheet on page 2) . . . | 5 | **0**

6 Additional amount, if any, you want withheld from each paycheck . . . . | 6 | $

7 I claim exemption from withholding for 2007, and I certify that I meet **both** of the following conditions for exemption.

- Last year I had a right to refund of **all** federal income tax withheld because I had **no** tax liability **and**
- This year I expect a refund of **all** federal income tax withheld because I expect to have **no** tax liability.

If you meet both conditions, write "Exempt" here . . . . ▶ | 7 |

Under penalties of perjury, I declare that I have examined this certificate and to the best of my knowledge and belief, it is true, correct, and complete.

Employee's signature
(Form is not valid
unless you sign it.) ▶ *Zoey Quigley*

Date ▶ *January 10, 2007*

8 Employer's name and address (Employer: Complete lines 8 and 10 only if sending to the IRS.)

9 Office code [optional]

10 Employer identification number (EIN)

Cat. No. 10220Q

Form **W-4** (2007)

For Privacy Act and Paperwork Reduction Act Notice, see page 2.

W-2 Form: A form prepared by your employer. It lists wages earned during that year, federal and state taxes withheld, and Social Security tax information. At the end of the year, use it to fill out your tax return.

GROSS PAY   FEDERAL DEDUCTIONS   STATE DEDUCTIONS

22222	a Employee's social security number	OMB No. 1545-0008		
b Employer identification number (EIN) 44-44556679	123-45-678	1 Wages, tips, other compensation 2,450.00	2 Federal income tax withheld 245.00	
c Employer's name, address, and ZIP code		3 Social security wages 2,450.00	4 Social security tax withheld 151.90	
Pizza Shack 1234 Workplace Street Hometown, NY 12345		5 Medicare wages and tips	6 Medicare tax withheld 35.53	
		7 Social security tips	8 Allocated tips	
d Control number		9 Advance EIC payment	10 Dependent care benefits	
e Employee's first name and initial Last name Suff.		11 Nonqualified plans	12a	
Zoey Quigley 678 Residence Avenue Hometown, NY 12345		13	12b	
		14	12c	
			12d	
f Employee's address and ZIP code				
15 State Employer's state ID number	16 State wages, tips, etc.	17 State income tax 98.00	18 Local wages, tips, etc.	19 Local income tax	20 Locality name

Form **W-2** Wage and Tax Statement

2007

Copy1—For State, City, or Local Tax Department

Department of the Treasury—Internal Revenue Service

where to put your money

where to put your money

"WE WERE ABLE TO FIND AN ACCOUNT OPTION THAT WAS RIGHT FOR ME."

Emma's Story

When Emma started baby-sitting last year, she had no idea how much her earnings would add up. "I was making a lot of money and keeping it in my dresser. My mom encouraged me to start keeping my money in a bank. So we went and opened a checking account."

With parental consent, Emma was able to begin banking her hard-earned bucks. "The woman at the bank sat with my mom and me and explained all my options. We were able to find an account option that was right for me. It has no minimum **balance** and no weird fees. And now I have a **debit card**, so it's really easy for me to get money when I need it, wherever I am."

Checking Accounts

Now that you actually have some money, it's time to bank it. Many banks allow people as young as 12 years of age to open checking accounts. A checking account is simply a bank account in which you have very easy access to your money. So what's the point of having one?

1. Safety: It's much safer to write a check or use an ATM or debit card than to carry cash. (More on ATM and debit cards later in this chapter.) If you lose your checkbook or card, all you have to do is let the bank know, and no one else can spend your money. If someone does spend your money before you report the card missing, you may be responsible for paying back a small amount of it, but that's a whole lot better than losing all of it!

2. Convenience: Checking accounts make life easier. In addition to writing checks to make purchases, you can use an ATM card at most bank machines. (But be careful of fees!) You can use a debit card for purchases anywhere credit cards are accepted.

3. Organization: With a checking account, someone else is helping you keep tabs on your money. Banks record every transaction—incoming and outgoing. Some banks also offer online banking, which allows you to check how much money you have in your account and to pay bills online.

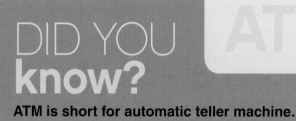

the
Early
BIRD

Debbie Pierce of Young Americans Bank in Denver, Colorado, told Scholastic *Choices* **magazine, "The earlier you start, the easier it'll be to manage your money later on."**

How to Choose a Checking Account That's Right For You

Not all checking accounts are created equal. There are lots of options, and they can be confusing. Start by heading to a few local banks (or looking up their Web sites) and collect information about all the different accounts they offer. Don't get overwhelmed! Take your time. Ask a bank employee questions if you're not sure you understand all the fine print. Once you've checked out the options from each bank you're considering, compare them and see which bank has an account that's best for you.

Look for key words like "free checking" or "student checking" to help you along. Usually these types of accounts are a safe bet. It's generally good for teenagers to have accounts that:

- have no fees or service charges. Some banks charge a monthly fee to keep your money. Other accounts may limit the number of checks you are able to write each month. If you go over that limit, there's a fee. And many banks have ATM/debit card charges. For example, if you **withdraw** money from another bank's ATM machine, your bank may charge you a fee. Those fees can add up to a lot of money, so steer clear of accounts that have them.

- don't have any minimum balance requirements. If you're like most teenagers, you won't always have constant cash flow. And you may want to spend it in large chunks, like to buy a car. Some checking accounts make you keep a minimum amount of money in the account at all times. If your balance falls below that minimum, you may be charged a fee. So, beware the minimum balance!

FREE **checking**
STUDENT checking

what to **BRING** when you **OPEN** the **ACCOUNT**

After you have chosen the checking account that makes the most sense for you, go back to the bank and get things rolling. You'll probably have to have a **parent or guardian** with you. You should both show up prepared with the **correct paperwork** and **identification**. Call the bank or check its Web site to find out what you'll need to bring.

how to read YOUR Bank Statement

Congrats!

You are the proud owner of your very own bank account. Okay, now what? Now you have to learn how to manage that account! Step one: understand your bank statements.

Once a month, your bank will send you a statement. That's a record of all the activity in your account that month. Here's a little help with understanding your statement:

FIRST BANK

9876 FINANCIAL ST
FORREST, MT 67899

CHECKING ACCOUNT STATEMENT
PAGE: 1 OF 1

JOE QUICK
123 FLOWER
FORREST, MT 67899

STATEMENT PERIOD	ACCOUNT NO.
4/5/2008 TO 5/4/2008	96385274

TRANSACTIONS

Date	Description	Withdrawals	Deposits	Balance
4/8/2008	DEPOSIT		109.55	581.97
4/13/2008	ATM WITHDRAWAL - 2ND BANK	-22.00		559.97
4/13/2008	ATM WITHDRAWAL FEE - 2ND BANK	-1.50		558.47
4/18/2008	CHECK NO. - 173	-15.20		543.27
4/19/2008	ATM WITHDRAWAL - FIRST BANK	-40.00		503.27
4/22/2008	DEPOSIT		109.55	612.82

ACCOUNT SUMMARY

PREVIOUS STATEMENT DATE	4/4/2008
BEGINNING BALANCE	472.42
DEPOSITS	219.10
WITHDRAWALS	77.20
FEES	1.50
ENDING BALANCE	612.82

STATEMENT PERIOD: The period of time that the statement covers, usually about a month.

TRANSACTIONS: Lists every time money went in or out of your account. Some banks will list deposits and credits in one place and withdrawals in another place.

ACCOUNT SUMMARY: A simplified version of the state of your account. It'll tell you the balance, deposits, checks, service charges, etc.

FEES: Your bank may charge you for a variety of things such as using another bank's ATM or ordering more checks. These may be listed separately or included in the list of transactions.

CHECKS: Checks that were processed are listed in numerical order. Some banks will even photocopy all the checks that were processed and enclose a copy with your statement.

ATM Cards Versus Debit Cards

An ATM card is a plastic card that looks like a credit card. It allows you to do the same things at a bank machine that you would at a bank. You can get cash, deposit money, check account balances, and receive a copy of your statement.

A debit card, or check card, is an ATM card with added benefits. It can be used as an ATM card, and it can also be used to buy things. Debit cards usually have the Visa or MasterCard logo on them, making them acceptable wherever credit cards are accepted. The amount you can spend is limited by the amount in your bank account. When you use a debit card to buy something, the business contacts your bank and automatically deducts the purchase amount from your checking account.

ATM smarts

- Keep your PIN (personal identification number) a secret—do not tell it to anyone.

- When entering your PIN, block anyone from seeing the keypad.

- Before you use an ATM, make sure it's in a safe, well-lit area.

THE PERKS
of debit cards

- Use it as an ATM card. Use a debit card to get cash or manage your checking account from any ATM.
- Use it to buy things. Using a debit card to make purchases is easier and faster than writing a check. And more businesses accept debit cards than checks.
- It's safer than cash. If you lose a debit card, contact the bank immediately, and they will replace it.
- It's safer than a credit card. You can't spend money that you don't actually have. So you can't get yourself into debt. (Be careful, though. Some debit cards offer automatic loans if you overdraft your account, so be sure to keep track of your spending. You could end up in debt without even realizing it!)

How to Write a Check

Step two in managing your checking account: dealing with checks. Checks are a way to transfer money from one person (you!) to another (the person, store, or service from which you are buying something).

Writing a check isn't hard, but there is a right way to do it:

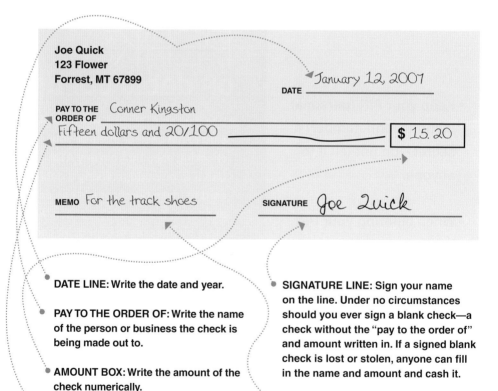

Joe Quick
123 Flower
Forrest, MT 67899

DATE _January 12, 2007_

PAY TO THE ORDER OF _Conner Kingston_

Fifteen dollars and 20/100 $ 15.20

MEMO _For the track shoes_

SIGNATURE _Joe Quick_

DATE LINE: Write the date and year.

PAY TO THE ORDER OF: Write the name of the person or business the check is being made out to.

AMOUNT BOX: Write the amount of the check numerically.

AMOUNT LINE: Start all the way to the left, and write the dollar amount in words. Then draw a line through any remaining blank space. This makes it more difficult for someone to alter the amount.

SIGNATURE LINE: Sign your name on the line. Under no circumstances should you ever sign a blank check—a check without the "pay to the order of" and amount written in. If a signed blank check is lost or stolen, anyone can fill in the name and amount and cash it.

MEMO LINE: This is a place where you can make a note to remind you and the person you're making the check out to what the check is for. If you're paying a bill that you have an account number for, such as cell phone service, put your account number on this line.

Keeping Track of Your Balance

The other responsibility that comes with a checking account is keeping track of your transactions and balance. You always want to be sure that your records match your bank's records.

There are two main reasons to keep tabs on this info:

 To be sure the people at your bank haven't messed up. They process hundreds or even thousands of transactions every day, and they're only human! So it's good to keep track of exactly how much you spent or deposited.

2 To be sure you know how much money is or should be in your account.

Checkbooks come with a check register, which is a booklet of pages with grids on them. The grid has blank spaces in which you write down every transaction you make—every time you write or deposit a check, swipe your debit card, or take cash from the ATM.

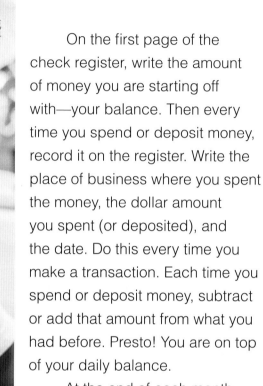

On the first page of the check register, write the amount of money you are starting off with—your balance. Then every time you spend or deposit money, record it on the register. Write the place of business where you spent the money, the dollar amount you spent (or deposited), and the date. Do this every time you make a transaction. Each time you spend or deposit money, subtract or add that amount from what you had before. Presto! You are on top of your daily balance.

At the end of each month, compare your register to the statement your bank sends you. If the transactions you wrote down don't match the ones your bank says you made, there could be a problem. Your bank may have made an error, and you'll have to give them a call to let them know.

Processing Time

One thing to remember is that money doesn't come out of your account the moment you sign a check or swipe your card. A check is only processed once the recipient deposits it. It can take time, as much as a week, to process. Only then will the money come out of your account. Debit card purchases can also take time to be processed. Be sure you keep track of your transactions. Your account balance at the ATM isn't always the whole story!

Cushion Yourself

Keep extra money in your account at all times. If you make a mistake, you want to have enough there to cover your error. "It's all about getting in the habit of saving and keeping track of your money. Little by little, you'll learn good habits which you'll need once you get a job and start paying your own bills," Debbie Pierce of Young Americans Bank in Denver, Colorado, told *Choices*.

"It's all about getting in the habit of saving and keeping track of your money."

Insufficient Funds

Aaron, 17, has his own debit card. But one day, that debit card came back to bite him. "I was on a date and was going to use my card to pay for dinner. I thought it would look cooler than paying with cash. So I acted all suave when the waitress brought the bill over. I just slipped her the card and said, 'Put it on this,' like my dad does at restaurants.

"But then she came back over and told me she couldn't take the card. She had put it through the machine, but there wasn't enough money in my bank account to cover the bill. My date had to pay. It was the worst!"

Even if you are incredibly careful about keeping track of your daily balance, you could still make a mistake here and there. If a transaction doesn't go through, you could have "insufficient funds." That means that you do not have enough money in your account to cover the expense. Or you could receive notice that you "bounced a check." This means the amount you wrote the check for is more than your balance. It usually carries a large fee (sometimes $35 or more!) and is also against the law.

But there's a way to avoid embarrassment, fees, or worse. Overdraft protection allows you to exceed your checking account balance without having to pay a huge fee. It's basically a loan that can come from a variety of places, including a savings account that you have linked to your checking account or a line of credit. Caution: Banks charge a fee for overdraft protection. Sometimes this fee can be quite high. So make sure you check into the details. Whatever you do, don't use overdraft protection like a loan! You'll get into debt that is very hard to pay off.

THREE out of **TEN** teenagers have checking accounts.

saving your money like a pro

saving your money like a pro

"IT'S REALLY AMAZING TO CHECK MY ACCOUNTS AND ACTUALLY WATCH THE MONEY GROW."

Shannon's Story

Shannon, 16, is a high-school sophomore who already has learned a lot about saving money for the future. "I've been working for a year for the family business. I think my parents realized that I wanted to be as successful as they are, so they told me how I could earn money from my money."

Shannon explains, "It's really amazing to check my accounts and actually watch the money grow. I'm so glad I had someone to help me learn this stuff now. I think it'll help me in the future. I will have enough money for a car when I'm ready for one. And I can help my parents pay for college."

Budgeting

There's no better way to see when and how you use money than to make a budget—a written plan for your money. Creating a budget is the best way to plan how to spend your hard-earned money.

On average, teens report having more than **$800** saved, whether that's at home, **in the bank**, or elsewhere.

Budgeting involves understanding how much money you earn and spend over a period of time—let's say a month. By subtracting what you spend each month from what you earn each month, you can see how much is left over. Tracking these amounts enables you to create a plan for spending—and saving your money.

teens on a
BUDGET

Only 13 percent of teens have ever made a budget. Of those who do, 39 percent update their budgets about once a month.

Teens who update their budget once a month

Teens who made a budget

Needs Versus Wants

The basic idea of budgeting is balancing needs versus wants. Shannon talked about her ideas on this: "I guess a *need* is something you can't do without, like maybe a house or a car. And a *want* is something that you can live without but would really like to have, like a vacation or maybe a designer bag."

Needs are the things you must have for survival. Many teens have parents who pay for these things now, but the older you get, the closer you come to having to pay for all of these things. On your own. It can be scary if you haven't really thought about it before. But that's what a budget is for! Examples of needs are gasoline, food, gas and electricity, rent, and medical **expenses**.

Wants are things you would like to have but that aren't required for your survival. You may not like it, but you could do without having them. Examples would be movie tickets, a video game, or even a cell phone.

"I guess a need is something you can't do without."

Fixed Expenses Versus Variable Expenses

Another important concept to understand before you start on your budget is fixed expenses versus variable expenses. This may sound like a mouthful, but the idea is simple. **Fixed expenses** are those that occur every month at the same amount—for example, a cell phone bill (as long as you don't go over your minutes!), rent, or a cable bill. With a fixed expense, you know how much money you will have to set aside each month to cover the costs.

The opposite of a fixed expense is a **variable expense**. These change from month to month, so it is a little harder to factor them in to your budget. However, many variable expenses, such as food or medical bills, fall in the needs category, so they have to be represented. Look over your spending for the past few months and estimate an amount that you'll need every month to cover each variable expense. It's better to set aside too much than too little.

PAY
YOURSELF
First

Many experts suggest that you should think of the money you put in savings as a fixed expense. This way, you are setting aside a specific amount before you even start thinking about how you want to spend the rest of your earnings. Decide how much you want to save each month, and put it into savings as soon as you get your paycheck. If you find that you have more than enough spending money during the month, you can increase the amount you save.

Worrywarts

Almost half of all teenagers say they sometimes worry about their finances. One in ten teens worries about them a lot.

Short-Term and Long-Term Financial Goals

A really important step in creating a budget for yourself is to figure out what you want to save up for. These are called financial goals. Some financial goals are considered short-term. Maybe you need a new pair of sneakers in time for track season, or perhaps you're dying to own a portable DVD player. In the grand scheme of things, these are not big-ticket items. They are things you could save for in a pretty short period of time—that's how they get their name, short-term goals.

Long-term financial goals are generally bigger-ticket items. They are goals for which it will take you longer to save. Examples of long-term financial goals include buying a car, traveling, or attending college (now that's a big-ticket item).

A Sample Budget

Let's take a look at an example of a budget so that you really get the picture of what short-term and long-term goals are and how to save for them.

1. **First, write down your monthly income.** Your monthly income is a combination of money you earn from working, money you are given as an allowance, and any other money you receive every month. Add up these different amounts to get your total monthly income and write it on line 1.

2. **Then write down your fixed monthly expenses.** These are things you have to pay for each and every month, without fail. Maybe it's your cell phone bill or bus fare. Include the amount you are setting aside for savings right off the bat. Add up these expenses, and write them on line 2.

3. Now subtract your fixed expenses from your income and write that number on line 3.

My Budget

The amount left over is what you have to cover both your variable expenses and

MY BUDGET	
total monthly income	$470.00
subtract fixed expenses	- $115.00
left over	$355.00

your wants. Once you have paid for the variable expenses, the rest of the money is yours to do with as you please. If you have some serious long-term spending goals, you should try to add a little extra to your savings every month on top of what you've already set aside.

Get More by Saving

You can see from the sample budget how to divide up your money to meet your financial goals. These goals may be short-term (you want a new computer or a pair of expensive jeans) or long-term (you want a car so bad you can taste it). Either way, you'll need to save your cash.

If your money is sitting in a savings account, it can actually grow into more money! The longer you have money saved, the better it is for you, because that money has more time to grow.

Okay, but how does that dollar become worth more in one year than it's worth today? When you deposit money in certain kinds of bank accounts, the bank actually pays you money. That money is called **interest**. The bank gives you interest for keeping your money there. And the more you save and the longer you save, the more interest you make.

INTEREST
in Action

This table will shed even more light on it for you:

To better understand what interest is and how it works to your advantage, it's easier to look at an example. One type of interest is called compound interest. Compound interest is when money grows over time, and the amount by which it grows increases every year.

For example, you start out with $100, and your annual interest rate is 5 percent. One year later, your $100 has grown by 5 percent. Five percent of $100 equals $5. If you add that to your original savings, you end the year with $105.

Year	Start with	Add 5%
0	$100.00	$5.00
1	$105.00	$5.25
2	$110.25	$5.51
3	$115.76	$5.79
4	$121.55	$6.08
5	$127.63	$6.38
6	$134.01	$6.70
7	$140.71	$7.04

The next year, your $105 earns another 5 percent in interest. But this time, you don't end up with $5. Five percent of $105 is $5.25. So at the end of the second year, you have $110.25 ($105 plus $5.25 equals $110.25).

Your initial $100 is growing, and the amount by which it's growing is also growing. Cool, huh?

Ways to Save: Savings Accounts

All right, you are starting to get the theory behind saving, right? You can make money on your money. Fantastic, but where do you put it to make it do that?

A safe way to save your money and have it gain interest is by putting it in a savings account. Saving accounts are "safe" because you aren't likely to actually lose any of your money in the process of making it grow. Because they are so safe, savings accounts pay a relatively low rate of interest.

- **Bank savings account:** Banks offer savings accounts as incentives for saving money—duh! With a bank savings account, you can make deposits and withdrawals, but you can't write very many checks, if any. Your money will earn a small amount of interest.
- **Money market account:** You will typically get a higher rate of interest here than in a savings account. However, you have to have a pretty high minimum balance (often $1,000) before you can start earning interest. There's often a service fee

if your balance falls below a certain level. Plus, these accounts have a limited number of withdrawals, which means you can't write many checks.

- **CD, or certificate of deposit:** With CDs, you agree to keep your money in an account for a specific amount of time. That can be anywhere from a few months to several years. Until your money reaches that date, you can't touch it, but the interest rates are better. If you do withdraw your money early, there is a penalty fee. So this type of account isn't for you if you think you might need the money before the time period ends.

THE NUMBER-ONE ITEM
teens are saving for?
Drum roll, please ... a car!
(Or car-related items.)

Ways to Save: Investing

Investing is another excellent way of saving your money. Investments are often considered less safe than traditional forms of saving, but they can pay off much bigger. If you're willing to invest for the long haul, it's usually worth the risk. There are many ways to invest your money, but the two biggies are in bonds and stocks.

- **Bonds:** A bond is basically an IOU. When a bond is issued, an investor—like you—agrees to loan money to a company or government. In exchange for lending your money, you are paid interest at a set rate for a set amount of time.

  Lend my money? It sounds crazy, but it can reap huge rewards. For example, say you buy a bond that's worth $10,000 now. You hold that bond for fifteen years. In fifteen years, the bond has "matured." So you get your $10,000 back, plus you've been getting significant interest payments every few months for that whole fifteen-year period.

  Other bonds, such as U.S. savings bonds, work differently. You buy a bond for one amount (say, $50), and it will be worth more (say, $100) when it matures.

PROS
AND CONS
of Bonds

THE GOOD:
- Bonds have higher interest rates than short-term investments (like CDs).
- Bonds are less risky than stocks.

THE BAD:
- Selling bonds before they mature will result in losing money.
- If the issuer of the bond (the person the investor lent the money to) declares bankruptcy, the investors could lose their money.

- **Stocks:** Stocks are shares of ownership in a company. When you invest in a company's stock or buy its shares, you are a shareholder. You own part of a company! A company's stock is determined by how many investors are interested in owning shares. If the company looks promising to other investors, your stock will increase in value.

   The buying and selling of stocks is handled by a **stock exchange**. The best-known stock exchanges in the United States are the New York Stock Exchange (NYSE), the American Stock Exchange (AMEX), and the National Association of Securities Dealers Automated Quotations system (NASDAQ).

Ways to Save: Retirement Saving

If you are like most teenagers, you're thinking, "Retiring? But I just started working!" This is true, but it's best to think of retirement accounts as the ultimate in savings. You are saving for the day when you can no longer work. And no work = no income.

   If you retire at the age of 65, you may live for decades with little money coming in. How are you going to live for that long with no savings? You can't, in spite of money you may receive from Social Security, so it's wise to start saving up now.

PROS
AND CONS
of Stocks

THE GOOD:

- Stocks have a long track record of earning more money than other forms of saving, such as money market funds, CDs, and bonds.
- Shareholders have some control. You get to vote for the company's board of directors, who represents the shareholders. They keep track of the important issues of the company.

THE BAD:

- Stock prices often go up and down. They are never guaranteed. So shareholders may lose part or all of their money.

- **IRA:** IRAs are the best way to start saving for retirement now. An IRA is an individual retirement account. The money isn't supposed to be removed until you're at or near retirement age.

  One advantage to many IRAs is that you will pay lower income taxes now. Why? The money you put into the IRA is taken directly from your income, so you end up paying taxes on the income that's left over. You can only put money into an IRA account if you have **earned income**—that is, if you worked for it.

  There are two types of IRAs to look into: traditional IRAs and Roth IRAs. Check out the Internal Revenue Service's Web site for more info: www.irs.gov/retirement/participant/index.html.

According to an article by finance pro Suze Orman of Yahoo! Finance, time is of the essence with retirement savings. "Consider that someone who starts socking away $300 a month at age 45, and earns an average annual return of 8 percent, will have about $178,000 at the age of 65. But if you start saving at 25, you'll have $1,054,000."

Save for Retirement?
NOW?

It might sound crazy, but it's never too early to start because the stats aren't working in your favor when it comes to retiring. In fact, an MsMoney.com study shows that among Americans 65 years or older:

22% must continue working

28% rely solely on welfare and Social Security

45% are dependent on their relatives

4% can meet their own expenses

1% have resources that exceed their living expenses

That means only 5% of all retired people are able to fund their own lives. So if you don't want to save, life after retirement will be difficult.

Source: www.msmoney.com/mm/investing/specific_goals/retirement.htm

spending
wisely

spending
wisely

"I CHARGED ALL OF IT BECAUSE IT FELT LIKE FREE MONEY."

Tara's Story

When Tara got her first credit card in her senior year of high school, she thought it was a big step toward financial freedom. What she didn't realize is that financial freedom requires financial responsibility. "I have been told a hundred times to be careful with my spending by my parents. But I always figured they were exaggerating, like they do whenever they don't want me to do something."

It didn't take long for Tara's spending habits to land her under a mountain of debt. "My last year of high school, I bought a lot of clothes, I went on spring break to Florida, and I went out to eat all the time. I charged all of it because it felt like free money. It felt like I wasn't really spending anything." All of that unwise spending put Tara in the hole to the tune of $3,500.

Unfortunately, Tara's story isn't unique. The appeal of spending money you don't really have is challenging even to adults. Many people get credit cards before they learn how to spend their money wisely. Spending money carefully can be just as important as saving it, because careful spending means avoiding unwanted debt.

Spending Versus Saving

Before spending a dime of your hard-earned money, take a minute to think about how badly you want what you're about to buy.

For example, 18-year-old Nancy says, "I swing by [a coffee shop] every morning before school and also before I go to work on weekends. I spend about $3.50 on a coffee. It's really not that much money. I mean, what else are you going to buy with $3.50?"

Well, let's see. Buying a cup of coffee every day may not seem like a big deal. But it's actually $1,277.50 a year (365 x 3.5). You can buy a lot with that money!

If Nancy invested that money in the stock market, she could earn about 12 percent per year. That would turn into about $2.44 million when she retires at age 65. Yes, that's right! If Nancy stopped buying coffee every day, she could end up with almost two and a half million dollars.

The same idea applies even when you're making once-in-a-while purchases. Chris, a high-school sophomore, says, "I just dropped about $600 on my [video game] system." If Chris had invested that money in the stock market, even for just five years, he could have had about $1,057.

You can see how if you spend money today, you are missing the opportunity to have more money tomorrow. So it's always better to really consider what you spend, every time you spend.

QUESTIONS
to Ask Yourself Before Buying

Why do you want the item?

Will you use the item more than once?

Will a different purchase make you just as happy?

What are the things you won't be able to do later if you make this purchase now?

How will this purchase affect your long-term financial goals?

Save While Spending

You may have noticed that the primary goal of this book is to encourage you to save. But let's be honest. You have to spend money sometimes. So if you must spend, spend wisely. Save as much as you can by shopping around and finding other ways to get the things you want.

Research before you buy. Look into the quality and reputation of the product or service. Check other stores or go online and compare prices.

Use coupons and rebates. If you know exactly what product you want, take advantage of store coupons and rebates.

Shop sales. A good time to look for sales is at the end of a season or a holiday.

Shop places other than the mall. Outlet stores offer good deals on designer stuff. Discount stores offer better prices for "staple" items, like pajamas and socks.

Online stores sometimes offer free shipping and discounted prices because they are competing against regular stores. There are even sites that do comparison shopping for you by showing you several different stores and the price at which they are selling the item you want. Check out sites like Froogle.com, Nextag.com, and Smarter.com.

Consignment or secondhand stores are usually careful about accepting only clothes in good condition. You can get some real buys there.

How SMALL savings add up

Saving a little here and a little there can be more useful than you think. Let's say you save $12 a week by buying sale items, cashing in rebate offers, and clipping coupons. After one year, you will have saved $624. You could probably find a use for that extra dough, couldn't you?

Credit Cards 101

Credit cards can be a great way to buy stuff when you don't have cash with you. But this convenience can come at a high price.

Here's how credit cards work. You make a purchase with your credit card. The credit card company then pays the store. Later, you'll get a bill in the mail or online from your credit card company for all the things you bought. You then have two choices: You can pay the bill in full, which is the best choice. Or you can pay a minimum amount—that is, put off paying the full amount until a later date.

However, if you just pay the minimum, the following month, the credit card company will charge you interest on the amount that you did not pay. That's how credit cards can create a nightmare of debt.

19%

Only 19% of teenagers say they are very familiar with how credit cards work.

Understanding How Credit Cards Work: Annual Percentage Rates

As Tara says about her credit card dilemma, "When I started getting credit card offers in the mail, I just accepted them without really reading or understanding all the details. So I opened accounts that had high [interest] rates and no perks. I didn't know anything about credit, really. So I didn't pay attention. I shouldn't have been charging things anyway, but at least if I had better [interest] rates on my cards, it would be costing me less to pay them off."

When you use a credit card, you are charged interest. Credit cards have an APR, which stands for annual percentage rate. This is the rate of interest being charged for the loan over a year. The APR rate includes interest, transaction fees, and service fees. Basically, the lower the APR, the better for you. Ten percent is considered a good rate.

"If I had better interest rates on my cards, it would be costing me less to pay them off."

Understanding How Credit Cards Work: Credit Card Traps

Credit card companies provide a service, but they also want to earn a profit. If you know what traps to avoid, credit cards can be really useful. But if you don't understand what you're getting yourself into, it's easy to get into a mess of debt.

- **Different APRs:**. Many credit cards have one APR for purchases, another for cash advances (when you use your card to get cash), and a third one for balance transfers (when you move debt from one card to another). The APRs for cash advances and balance transfers often are higher than the APR for purchases. Pay attention to how much interest your credit card company is charging you. Annual percentage rates change from year to year. Your credit card company must notify you if your APR changes, but that notification is likely in the fine print.

- **Teaser rates:** Many credit card companies offer low rates that last for a while. Key words: for a while. When the teaser rate period ends, your APR goes way up.

- **Late charges:** If the credit card company receives your payment after the monthly deadline, you will be charged a late fee. It's also likely that paying your bill late will make your APR skyrocket. (For example, many charge you $35 for being late. And your previous APR of 7.9 percent jumps up to 23 percent overnight.)
- **Annual fees:** Many credit card companies charge an annual fee. You have to pay them just for having their card. Sometimes you are billed for this each month; sometimes you're billed for the full amount once a year.

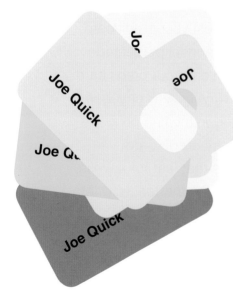

LIMIT
Your
Cards

Many people have as many as eight or nine different credit cards. That's an extremely bad idea. Limit yourself to one or two cards to keep yourself from getting in over your head.

Types of Credit Cards

Credit cards all look pretty much the same, but they carry different privileges and different responsibilities.

- **Prepaid credit cards:** With these cards, your parents transfer money from their checking accounts onto your card. Once you have spent that money, you can't use the card until more money is added. A small fee is charged for getting the card, but you do not have to pay any interest.
- **Low-limit cards:** With these cards, you can't spend more than a few hundred dollars before paying it off.
- **Low-interest cards:** These cards make carrying a balance into the next month less costly.
- **No-fee cards:** You are not charged an annual fee for having the card. These cards generally carry a higher interest rate.
- **Store cards:** Stores frequently offer their own credit cards. Many store credit cards provide their customers with coupons and information on upcoming sales, but they also tend to have high interest rates.

How to Get the Best Card for You

You must be 18 years old to apply for a credit card on your own, so if you aren't, you'll have to convince an adult that you're ready to have one. If you have consent, do some research to find the best offers. Search for rate comparisons at creditcards.com or MSN Money at moneycentral.msn.com. Good cards for teenagers are ones that:

- **have a low, consistent APR.** (Ten percent is pretty decent).
- **have no annual fees.**
- **have a low credit limit.**
- **have cash rewards.**
- **are prepaid.** (These are the best for teens. They teach you how to use credit cards responsibly, but carry a little less pressure).

What Using Credit Really Costs You

Before you use any credit card, even one with good rates, consider the cost at which that money is being "lent" to you. It's easy and tempting to use credit. But if you don't pay off more than the minimum balance on your card, every single thing you purchase ends up costing a lot more than its ticket price.

Here's an example. You go shopping and pick up a new video game console for $650. You also get a few games to go with it, so that's another $200. The holidays fall during the same month, so then you charge another $150 on gifts for your family. Before you know it, you have just charged a whopping $1,000 on your credit card.

You don't have enough cash to cover that bill—that's a lot of $$$! So you just pay the minimum amount due each time you get a statement. How long will it take to pay that off? Believe it or not, it could take you twelve long years to pay off if you only pay the minimum.

The real clincher here is total interest cost over those twelve years. The game console, games, and a few gifts (that you couldn't actually afford) just cost you almost $1,000 in interest!

Credit Card KARMA

Want to keep yourself out of trouble?

1 **Pay your bill.** You must pay at least the monthly minimum. Pay more if you can afford it, though! Your best bet is to pay the whole bill each month to avoid paying interest charges.

2 **Pay your bill on time, every time.** If you are late with a payment, you will have to pay a late fee. And they can be hefty. Another big downside to paying credit card bills late is that it negatively affects your credit score. (For more on credit scores, read the next section.)

3 **Avoid cash advances.** Most credit card companies offer cash advances, which is when they give you cold hard cash against your credit card limit. This is still a loan! And the interest rates charged for cash advances are typically much higher than those charged on purchases.

4 **Keep your card with you or in a safe place.** Inform the credit card company immediately if your credit card is lost or stolen. Someone could use your credit card to spend your money. Be sure you have the phone number of the credit card company handy in case your card is lost or stolen.

5 **Keep it private.** Do not give your credit card number to others, including friends.

6 **Check your receipts.** Before signing credit receipts for purchases, make sure you're being charged the right amount. Keep all receipts and check them against the billing statement. This will also help you monitor your spending.

7 **Don't lose control.** If your spending is out of control, cancel your card.

How to Keep Your Credit Cards in Good Standing

Regardless of the type of card you get, it's important to remember that you have just entered into a legal agreement with a credit card company. Legal, as in the law. That's serious! And it means that you have to take it seriously.

Understanding Your Credit Score

Every adult has what's called a **credit score**. Your credit score is a measure of your credit "worthiness." If you are very likely to repay debt, then you are considered "worthy" of credit.

If you have a low credit score, you won't be offered or approved for credit cards and won't be given loans for things like a car. But if your credit score is high, creditors will be more than happy to give you credit cards and offer you money to help you buy big-ticket items.

Your credit score is a measure of your credit "WORTHINESS"

WHAT
Your Credit Score Says About You

You now understand how your credit score is calculated, but what does it really mean? If you have a score of:

300–500:

501–619:

620–700:

700–800:

800 and above:

You have probably paid bills late a lot, and you have probably seriously messed up with a loan of some kind. Your credit is in very bad shape.

You have probably paid some bills late, but you're not in the worst possible shape.

You have a decent history of paying bills on time. But you may have missed a few and been charged late payments. You're not doing too bad and can usually get credit.

You are doing pretty darn good! You pay bills on time and manage your finances responsibly.

You are a credit prodigy. Put down this book and go work for an investment bank already!

How to Develop a Good Credit Score

As a teenager, there are three important steps to starting out on the right foot when it comes to credit:

1. **Establish credit history.** Open a credit card or get a loan for something big like a car (with a parent's consent and guidance). In a few years, you will have established a credit history.
2. **Pay your bill on time every month.**
3. **Pay more than the minimum amount due** on a credit card or loan. It costs you more in the long run if you don't, and you are proving to creditors that you aren't charging more than you can afford.

Credit NO-NO

According to her article "Boost Your Score," Kimberly Lankford reports that even something minor, such as overdue library books, can cause you big problems. If you don't pay the late fee to the library, your name is handed over to a "collections agency." A collections agency is a business that pursues payments on debts. Basically, employees there start bugging you to pay. Once you are "in collections," even for something as silly as library fines, your credit score will likely be lowered.

how debt is lost and found

how debt is lost and Found

"MY PARENTS JUST DON'T HAVE THE MONEY."

Shareef's Story

At age 18, Shareef is in debt for almost $30,000. How can that be? Not only is it possible, it's not as uncommon as you might think.

Shareef explains, "I started college this year and had to take out loans to afford it. My parents just don't have the money, and school is like $40,000 a year now. When my sister went to college in the '90s, it was less than $30,000 a year. But I have to go to college. The debt seems unavoidable."

Shareef also had a small amount of credit card debt when he entered college. "My parents let me open up a credit card account so that I'd start a credit history for myself. I am pretty good about it. I pay it on time and stuff, but that's another $500 right there that I owe someone. I don't even have a real job yet. And I can't get one until I finish college!"

Saving
for School

Among teens who save their money, 46% of them are saving it with the intention of paying the rising cost of college tuition.

What Is Debt?

All this talk of saving, spending, and credit comes down to one main concern: avoiding debt. Debt is money that is owed. Debt is created when someone loans you money. You have to repay loans—usually with interest added.

Millions of Americans have spent too much and learned the hard way how difficult debt can be to pay off. In fact, people currently in their twenties have the second-most debt in the country.

10

TEN Signs That You Are in Financial TROUBLE

1. You're always late paying your bills.
2. You often write checks for more money than you have in your checking account.
3. Your credit card accounts are usually at their maximum limits.
4. You apply for more credit cards because you have reached the limits on the ones you already have.
5. You are spending more than 20 percent of your income on credit card payments.
6. Your loan or credit card balances stay the same or get higher each month.
7. You can make only minimum payments on your accounts.
8. You don't have a savings account or have stopped making deposits into it.
9. You are always worried about your debts.
10. You use savings or credit cards to cover everyday living expenses, such as food.

How Did I Get Here?

Why are so many young Americans in debt? It depends on who you ask, but most financial experts agree it's due to the following:

- Credit card rates and fees
- High cost of college tuition
- Declining student grants for college
- Rising home prices

Half of all college graduates in 2004 had used credit cards for school expenses, according to the American Council on Education.

One out of every ten teens uses a credit card. By the time those teens enter college, their average debt on a personal credit card is about $1,500.

Good Debt Versus Bad Debt

While debt, in general, isn't appealing to people who are financially in the know, there is such a thing as good debt. Good debt is debt that can provide financial payoff. If you borrow money to buy a home, to pay for your education, or advance your career skills, this is considered good debt. You actually gain something profitable from having that debt.

But many people have what is called bad debt. Bad debt is built up when you borrow money for things that do not provide financial benefits, the way that college does. Bad debt comes from charging things that don't last as long as the length of the loan. If you borrow money for things like vacations or clothes, you are incurring bad debt.

when cash
counts

74%
**of teens agree that it's
very important to save
for college.**

63%
**of teens think it's necessary
to have money in order to
be successful in life.**

33%
**of teenagers think
money is important for
happiness.**

Getting Yourself Out of Debt

Shareef has started to understand how to go about paying off his debts. "I think I'm supposed to pay off the credit card first and then worry about the school loans later." Think he's right? Yup!

Credit experts agree that the best way to approach paying off debts is to:

1. **pay off bad debt first** and good debt second. When you evaluate what your bad debt is, pay off your highest interest rate debt first. Once the highest interest debt is paid off, start on the next highest.

2. **stop using your credit cards!**

3. **ask your creditors to reduce your interest rate.** Yes, you can do that! They may not want to do it, but it can't hurt you to try.

4. **ask for help from an outside source.** Contact the National Foundation for Credit Counseling (NFCC), a nonprofit organization that provides free and confidential debt management advice to anyone who needs it. For more information, head to www.nfcc.org.

If you have reached this page, you are well on your way to being financially educated. You know your APRs from your CDs, and the difference between income tax and earned income.

But what does all of this really mean? For starters, it means that you have just taken a huge step in empowering yourself to live a better life. The younger you are when you begin making good decisions about your money, the more benefits you will see from those decisions.

Even if you don't feel like a financial whiz kid right now, you know what you need to know to get a good start. So go forth and prosper!

balance—the difference between the original amount owed and the amount paid on the loan to date; alternately, it's what is left in an account after you deposit or withdraw money

bonds—investments in which you lend money to a corporation or government for a certain amount of time at a certain interest rate

certificate of deposit (CD)—a type of investment that requires you to invest money for a certain length of time and guarantees the same rate of interest for that entire period

compound interest—interest calculated on the amount originally invested and on any interest the investment has already earned

credits—money refunded to your bank account

credit score—the score a credit agency assigns you based on your ability to manage credit responsibility

debit card—a card you can use to pay for things directly from your checking account

deposit—to put money into a checking, savings, or other investment account

earned income—wages paid in exchange for work

entrepreneurs—people who take risks and start businesses in hopes of making a profit

expenses—things you pay for

fixed expenses—expenses that stay the same from month to month

income tax—money paid to the government each year by workers

interest—the amount paid for the privilege of borrowing money; alternately, the amount earned by savers as incentive for saving money

investing—putting your money into accounts, businesses, or property that you hope will grow in value and earn a profit

savings account—a bank account that pays interest for keeping your money there

stock exchange—a central market where brokers buy and sell shares of stock

variable expenses—expenses for which the amount you pay varies from month to month

withdraw—to take money out of an account

Books

Cathers, Ben. *Conversations with Teen Entrepreneurs: Success Secrets of the Younger Generation.* Lincoln, NE: iUniverse, 2003.

Fischer, Jeff. *The Motley Fool's Investing without a Silver Spoon: How Anyone Can Build Wealth Through Direct Investing.* Alexandria, VA: Motley Fool, 1999.

Shelly, Susan. *The Complete Idiot's Guide to Money for Teens.* Indianapolis: Alpha Books, 2001.

Online Sites & Organizations

CU Succeed Network
www.cusucceed.net

Federal Deposit Insurance Corporation (FDIC)
www.fdic.gov

Federal Reserve Board
www.federalreserve.gov

Internal Revenue Service (IRS)
www.irs.gov

The Jumpstart Coalition
www.jumpstart.org

The Motley Fool
www.fool.com

Office of the Comptroller of the Currency (OCC)
www.occ.treas.gov

Students.gov
www.students.gov

U.S. Department of Labor
www.dol.gov/esa

Young Investor
www.younginvestor.com

Young Money
www.youngmoney.com

About the Author

Danielle Denega is an author of books for children and young adults. Her other nonfiction titles for Scholastic include *Gut-Eating Bugs*, *Skulls and Skeletons, Have You Seen This Face*, *The Cold War Pigeon Patrol and Other Spy Animals*, *A Reading Guide to Julie of the Wolves*, *A Reading Guide to Sarah, Plain and Tall*, and *Let's Read About ... Betsy Ross*.

In addition, Ms. Denega has written more than twenty other books for young people. She has a bachelor's degree in English and makes her home in Charlottesville, Virginia, with her husband, Brian, and their dogs, Quigley and Zoey.